HERMAN®
OVER THE WALL
THE SEVENTH TREASURY

Other Popular Herman Books

The 1st Treasury of Herman
The Second Herman Treasury
Herman, The Third Treasury
Herman: The Fourth Treasury
Herman Treasury 5
Herman: The Sixth Treasury
"Herman, You Can Get in the Bathroom Now"
"Herman, Dinner's Served...As Soon as the Smoke Clears!"
"Herman, You Were a Much Stronger Man on Our First Honeymoon"
The Latest Herman
"They're Gonna Settle Out of Court, Herman"

HERMAN®
OVER THE WALL

THE SEVENTH TREASURY

by Jim
Unger

Andrews and McMeel
A Universal Press Syndicate Company
Kansas City • New York

Herman® is syndicated internationally by Universal Press Syndicate.

Herman Over the Wall: The Seventh Treasury copyright © 1990 by Universal Press Syndicate. All rights reserved. Printed in the United States of America. No part of this book may be used or reproduced in any manner whatsoever without written permission except in the case of reprints in the context of reviews. For information write Andrews and McMeel, 4900 Main Street, Kansas City, Missouri 64112.

ISBN: 0-8362-1819-1
Library of Congress Catalog Card Number: 90-82672

EDITOR & PUBLISHER for February 10, 1990

'Herman' comic in East Germany

"Herman" by Jim Unger of **Universal Press Syndicate** is now appearing in East Germany.

"There have been other comic features sold to magazines in the Eastern bloc, but 'Herman' will be the first to appear in newspapers," believes **Editors Press Service** president John P. Klem. "This is definitely an important step — real evidence that the Berlin Wall has crumbled."

Klem, whose company handles international distribution for Universal, said Unger's panel is being published by *Norddeutsche Zeitung* in Schwerin and *Ostsee-Zeitung* in Rostock. The East German papers join over 350 other "Herman" clients in about two dozen countries, including the U.S.

HERMAN

by JIM UNGER

"You're OK. How am I?"

"You'll have to return to your seat, sir...
we can't keep circling the airport."

"Why do you *always* have to make a
contest out of everything?"

"Dimitri, 'punch' is a type of fruit drink."

10

"Yes, yes, I know you were excited. But read it yourself. It says, 'Head man wanted for branch office.'"

"We've genetically engineered a tuna exactly the same diameter as our cans."

"Sorry about all the noise, Mr. Robertson. The gentleman is here who invented the eight-foot television."

"Young man, has it occurred to you that you'll be boiling a young, innocent creature that would have had the potential for a full and productive life?"

"It happened during one of those used-car-dealer commercials."

"If you touch that nerve again, I'm gonna teach you a new meaning for the word *pain.*"

"Sure, you were good at it. You were *there* for most of it."

"I can't see it. Look in your pockets."

HERMAN

by JIM UNGER

"Oh, that's nice. It says, 'Our company took every precaution to see that the pig didn't suffer.'"

"I suppose you realize that behind your back Mom calls you 'chicken legs.'"

"The *dog* ate a whole bag of chili powder."

"Who put in that crown?"

"You're *supposed* to be holding it *straight!*"

"I'd like to return this mink. My husband bought it for my birthday as a little joke."

"You should never stifle a sneeze!"

"I wish you hadn't told the waiter he didn't look his age."

"He said he hates to be a bother, but could you please sharpen this up for tomorrow's battle."

"Personally, I *prefer* a soft mattress."

"OK, a cheeseburger for you. What about the Statue of Liberty over here?"

HERMAN

"Clarissa, will you please get back in here
this instant."

"I lost 10 pounds once. To be honest, I
didn't notice any difference."

"He can't see you for at least
three weeks."

"It's been road-tested."

"Your honor, if my client is found not guilty, he could lose more than $2 million in book royalties alone."

"Stay away from that cake in the fridge."

"Room service."

"How many times have I told you about running in the corridors?"

"Hey, poodle...sweetheart....How's it going, baby?"

WOULDN'T YOU RATHER BE SHOPPING?

HERMAN

by JIM UNGER

"Pepper?"

"I gotta be straight with you, Andrea. I wear special shoes to make me look taller."

"You should be careful with blisters. You'd better let the doctor take a look at it."

"Mom, is this my baby sitter?"

"Dad, I can't find my baseball anywhere."

"Your cousin Ernie failed his skydiving course."

"License."

"It's not as bad as it looks."

"His brother and his nephew Reggie are doing 12 years for armed robbery."

"Grandma, can you lend me $11 to get a set of false fingernails?"

"Rapid pulse, sweating, shallow breathing.... According to the computer, you've got gallstones."

"Listen, friend, if you wanna date my daughter, you'd better start letting your hair grow."

HERMAN

by JIM UNGER

"No wonder you're having difficulty walking. You've got an armchair back here!"

ART SUPPLIES

"Where can I get a bunch of sunflowers?"

"Who d'you think wants to drink that after *you've* been sitting in it?"

"You promised me you'd get a haircut."

"Well, now we know what they meant when they said, 'You can't take it with you.'"

"It's nearly 1989, G.B. We have to move with the times. My salesmen need horseless carriages."

"I bought her a cookbook the day we got married.... It's still in the wrapper."

"Who are you gonna vote for, Mike Bush or George Dukakis?"

"I thought you said they'd fixed this thing!"

"They're all the same.... As soon as I laid the egg, he was off."

"What's going on? Everyone told me I couldn't bring it with me!"

"I got them both during
mating season."

HERMAN

by JIM UNGER

"When we get short of bed space, we walk around the wards with it."

"Watch the movie, Kevin. You don't want to ruin your chances of ever becoming a TV evangelist."

"Whaddyer think it is?"

"What am I...48? That's the first time I noticed my knees bend the other way!"

"Are you thinking what I'm thinking?"

"Mr. Picasso, I'll be able to work only a half-day Thursday."

"If I pay this amount of taxes, I'll qualify for tax exemption as a non-profit organization!"

"I understand Albert Einstein spent most of his life trying to get elected."

"Which way do you think it's facing?"

"Are you sure it's dead?"

"I'm studying astrophysics and you're reading me 'Goldilocks and the Three Bears'!"

"You can call me apathetic if you like. See how much I care!"

HERMAN

by JIM UNGER

HEAR THAT?

A SCRUNCHING NOISE!

THERE IT GOES AGAIN! WE'VE GOT RATS!

WHERE'S THE LIGHT!

35

"Sweetheart, don't forget your school lunch."

"I'm only really happy when I'm miserable."

"I warned you about pulling out gray hairs."

"My first husband, George, loved to fly."

"I guess you could say I'm a self-made man."

"I had to give everyone their money back!"

"I'm sorry, slr. You sald you wanted the cheapest room."

"Gentlemen, to combat the growing menace of VCR machines, I think we in television should restrict ourselves to no more than 45 minutes of advertising in any given hour of programming."

"I don't think Mom makes spaghetti on toast like that."

"Take that out of your mouth and tell the nice man why you'd like a job here."

"This is the 11th time I've sent you to prison. You haven't learned much in 30 years, have you?"

"If I can't spell it, how can I look it up in the dictionary?"

HERMAN

by JIM UNGER

BIG MOUTH.

YOU'RE THE ONE WHO TOLD HIM NOT TO SHOW HIS FACE AROUND HERE AGAIN UNTIL HE GOT A HAIRCUT AND A JOB...

YOU TOLD HIM HE WAS A 'LAY-ABOUT'...

I COULD HEAR YOU TWO FROM DOWN THE STREET.

WHAT'S GOING ON?

HIS BROTHER WON $6 MILLION IN A LOTTERY.

"My doctor told me to take a cruise and relax."

"I'm taking you off the vitamins for a while."

"Got the waterproof matches?"

"What's it like for cornering?"

"He stole $15 million, your honor, and he
wants to plead 'guilty with
an explanation.'"

"We just don't see eye to eye anymore."

"He'd just spent $600 having his tooth capped."

"We the jury find the defendant not guilty by reason of insanity."

"You won't find it under 'plumber.' Look under 'drain surgeon.'"

"How often do you find a basement apartment with a balcony?"

HERMAN

by JIM UNGER

"Quit fooling around!"

"I don't know what this is, but you need a new one."

"Is this allowed?"

"They're specially bred for long walks."

HOTEL

"The honeymoon suite is booked for another 20 minutes."

"I need something with controls in the back seat."

"It'll speed things up if you order the meatloaf."

"You'll be hearing from my lawyer."

"I need a pair of dancing shoes with steel-toe caps."

"Since she got her new teeth, she's put on 60 pounds."

"'Catch of the Day' is fish fingers."

"In 10 years, she's gone from ballerina to sports arena."

HERMAN

by JIM UNGER

"I can get time off for bad behavior."

"I'm tired of being an unknown artist."

"My birthday surprise was walking into the kitchen and finding the toaster on fire."

"It keeps the bag-snatchers away."

"If you're thinking of wishing me a happy birthday, it was *last week!*"

"On a scale of 1 to 10, she's a light heavyweight."

"It's a very popular gift item for $15. We put a $95 price tag on it."

"What's the get-well card for?"

"We got any *white* salmon?"

"He loves people. But mostly he gets canned dog food."

"These pills are a dollar each, or you can take two for $1.50."

HERMAN

by JIM UNGER

51

"If she doesn't show, d'yer wanna come to Niagara Falls?"

"I don't want to worry you, but the guy who delivered the pizza was your financial planner."

"He thinks a chiropractor is an Egyptian doctor."

"I get a real deal on fire insurance."

"This Beef Wellington tastes like rubber boots!"

"We went to Greece for a second honeymoon. Six days and seven fights."

"My life insurance company has offered me a reduction if I eat out."

"We haven't had a contract since 1742!"

53

"It's his first time."

"Dino doesn't like pizza."

"So this is your private box at
the theater!"

"It's for my mother-in-law. Got
anything rabid?"

HERMAN

by JIM UNGER

"It's an emergency. She's gotta be at the hairdresser in three minutes."

"I gotta leave you on your own for a few weeks."

"Someone stole his elevator shoes."

"Here's your supper. I've waxed the floor."

"Extraterrestrials have landed."

"My ex-husband was up all night buying everybody drinks."

"If you're bored, go home."

"Is that all you have to say in your defense?"

"I thought my shoe was squeaking."

"My teacher assures me that even though I have your nose and eyes, genetics have absolutely nothing to do with the brain."

"Get me to the airport in 10 minutes and I *may* overlook this filthy cab."

"She gave me aftershave for Christmas,
so I gave her beauty soap."

"I'm just going over to the bowling alley to
get a candy bar."

"Sure I'll take you out to dinner! Which
two restaurants?"

"I can't wait to open your suitcase!"

"After you've finished the baby, I'd like to change my name to 'Lance.'"

"I always sit behind her on the bus in case there's a head-on collision."

"I thought you said you were in shipping."

"No, thanks. I couldn't take your last nickel."

"I wanna buy a book about the universe."

"Wanna take it for a test push?"

"This is the best I can do for 'previous employment.'"

"This reading lamp hasn't uttered a word since I bought it!"

"Special delivery."

"Have a cup of coffee while I'm getting ready."

"Did you have to buy him such a
big bucket?"

"He was born on the second and third
of December."

"She went to see a hypnotist to lose
weight and he put on 40 pounds."

"I don't want to rush things. Let's exchange photographs first."

"I missed the gas pedal."

"I brought your slippers."

"Simpkins, how many times have I told you about using the office paper-shredder to make cole slaw?"

HERMAN

by JIM UNGER

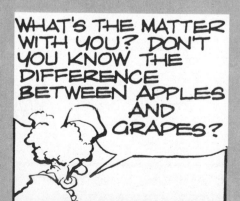

"A lot of men would *love* to be 7 feet tall."

"He starts barking when the mailman leaves the depot."

"How much would it cost to send a 185-pound wooden crate to Hawaii for two weeks?"

"For the last *&*% time...over the wire fence is *not* a home run."

"We'll get you down to X-ray in a few minutes."

"You'd look a lot better if you didn't wear a striped shirt."

"The fridge stopped working, so I put antifreeze in the milk."

"I wanted to get you a gift you deserved, but they didn't have anything cheaper!"

"It's nothing to worry about, but I want you to wear this Medic-Alert helmet."

"It serves him right. He's bitten the valve off my tire."

"He's been driving 16 hours non-stop."

HERMAN

by JIM UNGER

DID YOU SEE THIS?

IT SAYS HERE THAT 98% OF ALL FIRST OFFENDERS ATTENDED SOME SCHOOL....

...97% HAD TIGHT SHOES AS A CHILD.

94% PARENTS QUARRELED.

92% HAD SOME RELIGIOUS TRAINING.

86% READ PORNOGRAPHY.

85% LIVED WITH AN INCESSANT TALKER.

"Mother asked me to get you to open this jar of pickles for her."

"Excuse me. May I go ahead of you? I'm in rather a hurry."

"Say, aren't you Harry Henderson and Pete Watson?"

"I can't remember which one of these is fish and chips and which one is liver and onions."

"His doctor told him to stay away from anything fatty."

"We've been married for 27 years. How about time off for good behavior?"

"Which hospital did you stay at on your honeymoon?"

"Needless to say, we don't buy the extra-large eggs anymore."

"Eighty years old and he doesn't have a gray hair on his head."

"Are you steering?"

"He says he's invented a saltshaker that will never clog."

"He's taking one of those correspondence courses to become a window dresser."

HERMAN

by JIM UNGER

"Most of them are for ballroom dancing."

"Looks like 'zebra' finally made it onto the endangered list."

"I didn't say 'undress.' I said 'address.'"

"You get a company car after two years."

"You call yourself 'early man'! You're three hours late!"

"The guarantee ran out while you were on the phone."

"I heard you played by ear."

"I wonder if they'll remember you."

"Take me to the best restaurant in town and leave the engine running."

"This will all be yours one day, Darryl."

"Send the speeding ticket to the car lot. I'm not buying it."

"I'd like to bury your daughter."

HERMAN

by JIM UNGER

"He's looking for something for the
woman who has nothing."

"She wants to know what the pot roast
was like."

"Boo-oo-oo-ots."

"She just had her physical. The doctor says she's as fit as a double bass."

"It's just as 'Goldie' left it four years ago today."

"Come back and see me in two weeks, and don't wear that tie."

"If I give myself up, do I get to keep the money?"

"Wouldn't I get faster service if I slept in your room?"

"That rotten dog made me a birthday card!"

"Personally, I think it helps the divorce if we leave *both* of them in there."

HERMAN

by JIM UNGER

"It's a romantic novel . . . pure escapism."

"I taught him everything I know and he's still stupid."

"There's a bottle of wine on here that's more than our mortgage payment!"

"He's always had a vivid imagination."

"Apart from the words 'orange-flavored chooey choo,' the rest is in Latin."

"I wouldn't pay all that for a dress while you're still growing."

"Just been to see his schoolteacher."

"Have you got that book, 'How to Be Six Feet Tall Under Hypnosis'?"

"What's it like, being inside there?"

"They're gonna settle out of court."

"Stand back, everybody. He thinks he's a frog."

"She's the only one who can eat her own cooking."

"NOT GUILTY," YOUR HONOR.

THIS IS RELIGIOUS PERSECUTION, YOUR HONOR. I BELONG TO A SMALL BUT VERY DEVOUT SECT.

WHAT'S THAT GOT TO DO WITH ALL THESE UNPAID PARKING TICKETS?

THIRTY-EIGHTH COMMANDMENT!

WHAT ABOUT IT?

THOU SHALT PARKETH THINE OWN CHARIOT OUTSIDETH THINE OWN HOUSE.

"About 150 miles. What about you?"

ELEPHANT HOUSE

"They've decided it *was* a job-related accident."

"My school report card is not going to help your ulcer."

VET.

"I've done the best I can."

90

"Sorry I left during your sermon. I was sleepwalking."

"Money or good looks attract me. I'd say you'd need about $15 million."

"He said I don't need glasses!"

"See what happens when you can't make up your mind?! ... 'Illegal U-Turn.'"

"Well, at least she got it out of her system."

"Whaddyer mean, 'They don't look like you'? You *idiot*. They're *eggs!*"

"It doesn't bother you if I eat while you're smoking that big cigar, does it?"

"Whaddyer mean, 'I burnt the oatmeal'? ...that's coffee!"

HERMAN

by JIM UNGER

"Now, why on earth wouldn't you tell me you were allergic to penicillin?"

"We've been married more than seven months now, Beryl. Shouldn't you be ironing or something?"

"Did you know that no two cornflakes are identical?"

"We've just walked two miles...that's 14 for him."

"I'm gonna pay my electricity bill while I'm here."

"That used to be my best subject. Ask me the capital of Spain."

"I'm only helping with the dishes 'til you get your pacemaker."

"If I keep to the speed limit I'll never get airborne."

"Our marriage was built on mutual trust and a lot of acting ability."

"D'you believe this guy. That's six times in a row he's grabbed the check!"

"All your tests were negative...which is positive."

"I'm in the dry-cleaning business."

WHAT A BREAK!

IT'S HIS FIRST DAY.... HE WAS SO EXCITED... HE'S BEEN OUT OF WORK FOR EIGHT MONTHS.

$385 A WEEK IS GONNA MAKE A BIG DIFFERENCE AROUND HERE.

WHY'S HE SITTING OVER THERE READING THE NEWSPAPER?

THEY SENT HIM HOME EARLY.

THEY'RE ON STRIKE FOR MORE PAY.

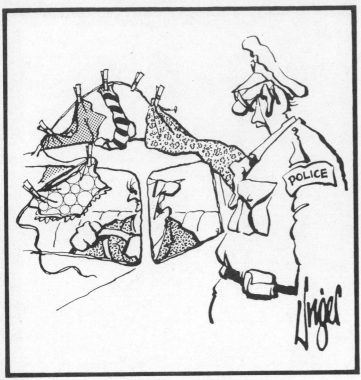

"What is it this time?"

"Looks like I'll be playing the ninth hole and you're playing the 13th."

"I wonder if they spray chemicals on macaroni."

"He may be an Indian, sir, but he's a superb tactician."

"I prefer to work without supervision."

"The kitchen sink is all greasy."

"It's so damp in our room, her wedding ring's turned green!"

"I hope you're not one of those people who have trouble swallowing pills."

"You know what they say, 'Two can starve as cheaply as one.'"

"He gets those sudden migraines."

"Whadda you think of gun control?"

"No, no, no. Point to Africa on the globe."

ARE YOU FEELING OK?

WHY ARE YOU LOOKING SO SERIOUS?

OH, I DON'T KNOW... I WAS JUST THINKING ABOUT HOW NONE OF US IS GETTING ANY YOUNGER.

WHAT BROUGHT THIS ON?

GEORGE IS IN THE DEN, IN FRONT OF THE TELEVISION.

WATCHING OPERA.

"She coulda been Miss Universe on any other planet."

"The doctor's put him on a vegetarian diet . . . like an elephant."

"Can't you go faster?"

"How are you gonna defend me if you can't stop laughing?"

"I gotta get new glasses."

"This is a video of you two watching the video of our vacation."

"It's a type of palm."

"D'you wanna speak to the boss or to someone who knows what she's talking about?"

"I've got to get an early start in the morning."

"Divorce is very hard on the goldfish."

"That is *not* the way to pass the potatoes!"

"Hello, Harry ... it's me."

HERMAN

by JIM UNGER

"She's the opposite of 'anorexic.'"

"She's very quick with a potato peeler."

"Corned beef hash... white meat only."

"We offer the most limited warranty in town."

"Who d'you think's paying for all this?"

"His doctor told him to cut out sugar."

"Find out how much to fix it. Take it to three different toy stores."

"You don't have to stop at red lights."

"Hey, Pops, d'you think you can make the airport by Tuesday?"

"I can start work Monday if I don't win the lottery."

"Don't go in the kitchen."

"The first number ... is ... five."

by Jim Unger

HERE'S A NEWS BULLETIN...

DUE TO A BREAKDOWN IN SALARY NEGOTIATIONS...

DUE TO A BREAKDOWN IN SALARY NEGOTIATIONS...

BETWEEN MYSELF AND THIS NETWORK...

BETWEEN MYSELF AND THIS NETWORK...

AFTER NINE YEARS...

AND MUCH SOUL-SEARCHING...

I'VE DECIDED TO QUIT MY JOB!

"Donald Trump's thinking of buying South America."

"These are my two references; neither of them can write."

"She hates to part with it."

"If you'll allow me, sir, I'd recommend the cheese salad and a very substantial tip."

"As a matter of fact, I went to all this trouble just to say 'I don't.'"

"OK, but only until I find someone better."

"In a few minutes, you're going to meet two nice gentlemen dressed in white coats."

"He's never far from his stamp collection."

"There wasn't any space left for the vodka."

"There's a surgeon general's warning on the potatoes."

"For the first week, I think you should leave 20 minutes apart."

"D'you take plastic?"

by Jim Unger

GET YOUR FATHER ON THE PHONE...

IS THAT YOU, RANDOLPH?... LISTEN, I'M DOWN AT CITY HALL PICKETING SO YOU'LL HAVE TO DO THE GROCERY SHOPPING FOR ME.

STOP POLLUTION

GOT A PENCIL?...YEAH...GET ME A LARGE DETERGENT AND A BOTTLE OF BLEACH...A TUBE OF SHAMPOO AND SOME FABRIC SOFTENER. ALSO, WE NEED A CONDITIONER.

STOP POLLUTION

I NEED TOILET BOWL CLEANER AND SOME SPRAY-ON OVEN CLEANER.

STOP POLLUTION

THEN GO TO THE HARDWARE SECTION AND GET A GALLON OF PAINT THINNER.

STOP POLLUTION

...AND IF YOU'RE GOING TO DO THE LAWN OVER THE WEEKEND, WE WANT WEED KILLER.

STOP POLLUTION

115

"They had a retirement party for me, and I was the only one not invited!"

"I'm sorry, sir, there's no shaving in the restaurant."

"It's OK, officer. She's looking for the emergency brake."

"You may as well drink, Angela, because there's no way you're driving."

"Table by the window, please."

"I'm not really overqualified. My resume is a pack of lies."

"The zoo has decided *not* to press charges."

"Freedom."

"We pool our tips here. What's 50 cents divided by 27?"

"He uses that one when he can't find his false teeth."

"He won't go out with anyone except my wife."

COME IN, CRUDLEY.

CRUDLEY, THIS IS YOUR FOURTH YEAR AT THIS MEDICAL COLLEGE.

...AND I HAVE HERE YOUR HAND-WRITTEN EXAMINATION PAPERS.

NO ONE CAN UNDERSTAND A SINGLE WORD OF IT.

IT IS TOTALLY ILLEGIBLE.

WELL DONE.

119

"Each hour."

"We sleep in separate bedrooms mainly to prevent the house from tipping over."

"Lifetime guarantee against speeding tickets."

"You can guess who's paying for this lot ... 'wedding doughnuts.'"

"Thirty-five thousand feet, one way."

"Hey, waiter. We'll share a medium pizza."

"Don't drive around like that! Find
a gas station!"

"Do you mind telling me why there are
carpet fibers on this sausage?"

"Kid, it's against the law to tell people you're 50 years old."

"Imagine anyone planting a tree right there!"

"Got him!"

"The typesetters are on strike."

HERMAN

by JIM UNGER

"If you could afford the fare, I'd suggest Brazil."

"How much?"

"Cruise control."

"I've just calculated that by the year 2183, the government will declare the 365th national holiday."

"You'll need this for the steak and kidney pie."

"I wonder if there's intelligent life on other trees."

"Will you do both of us for $5?"

"The odd-numbered caves are on the other side of the gorge."

"One day you're gonna be really happy you bought that life insurance."

"When we get more members, we'll buy a bigger piece of land."

"A what?"

HERMAN

by JIM UNGER

"Experience! Are you kidding? I've had 12 jobs this year alone!"

"I hope you're not going to be like my first three husbands. They all went bankrupt."

"There's a limit of one per customer."

"This one's 10 percent real food."

"You go ahead of me. I think you're faster."

"He'll only go on the rug."

"I went straight from a broken home to a fixed income."

"I've got a very sensitive nose."

"As it's your birthday tomorrow, we've all decided to close up and have the day off."

"You never seen a ham operator before?"

"I'm sorry, sir. Dr. Rogers can see you only by referral."

WHAT ARE YOU IN FOR?

I GOT THREE MONTHS FOR ASSAULT WITH A DEADLY WEAPON.

A GUNMAN TRIED TO ROB MY STORE ...I THREW THE CASH REGISTER AT HIM AND BROKE HIS HAND.

HIS LAWYER SAYS HE WON'T BE ABLE TO HOLD A GUN WITHOUT A LOT OF PAIN FOR AT LEAST SIX MONTHS.

...SO NOW HE'S GOT A CIVIL JUDGMENT AGAINST ME.

...LOSS OF INCOME.

"I warned you about taking steroids with your low blood pressure."

KITCHEN APPLIANCES

"It woke me up two hours late with a cold cup of coffee."

"Can I use your phone?"

"I'd say they're about the most pathetic fantasies I've ever heard."

"I hope this divorce lasts longer than your last one."

"We're not trying to see your house; we're selling the planet."

"Remember the good old days when the railway porter used to put down a little wooden step to help you get off the train?"

"You told me to hang your mother's picture in the hallway."

"He was trying to fill a disposable lighter."

"Hand over all the french fries, you dirty rat."

"I hate to leave without buying *something.*"

"I told you to fetch me a *sander.*"

136

137

"You're being charged with 'disturbing the ambience.'"

"This is my husband, the last of the big suspenders."

"Let's try once more. We could get lucky the third time."

WHAT HAVE YOU GOT TO LOSE?

50¢

"Gimme a gin and lettuce."

"He painted that one on our camping trip."

"They said you were wearing this when you fell off the roof."

"The 50-cent surcharge is for the clean fork I brought you when you dropped the other one."

"It's too tight."

"You ordered a small Pisa."

"Today's special is spaghetti with alphabet letters in the sauce."

"Dad, if you let me have a credit card, I *swear* I'll never use it."

by Jim Unger

WHAT HAVE YOU TO SAY FOR YOURSELF?

YOU HAVE 16 PREVIOUS CONVICTIONS!

YOUR HONOR, I REMEMBER LEAVING SCHOOL WHEN I WAS 15, BUT AFTER THAT, EVERYTHING IS A BLANK.

THIS THROWS A NEW COMPLEXION ON THE WHOLE CASE.

I'M ORDERING A PSYCHIATRIC EXAMINATION.

FOR YOU OR FOR HIM?

"You can get down now. That was your raise."

"If you run like the wind, you may just make it."

"I've lost the use of my left arm."

"They had baseball back then?"

"The doctor said you had a 50-50 chance."

"My sister TOLD me you were no good."

"You should see the pills I have to take."

"He took out my appendix and I haven't got a scar."

"This one was driven by a little old lady and her nephew."

"I want to report an unidentified flying omelette."

STOP LOSING YOUR HAIR

HERMAN

by JIM UNGER

"I keep going hot and cold."

"Bagel!"

"Terrible thing, depression."

"He doesn't get THAT from his father."

"All right, all right...Hand over seven bucks."

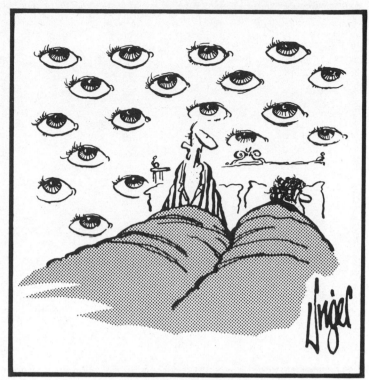

"It's no use. I can't sleep with this wallpaper."

"You can get up now."

"I've decided to expand my horizons."

"My little TV's not working."

"Where did you buy those boots?"

"We're under new management. 'Soup of the day' is a mushroom omelet."

"Remember six years ago when you left the gate open?"

HERMAN

by JIM UNGER

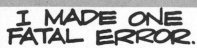

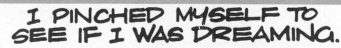

"I don't like to get personally involved."

"We don't want to confuse the public."

"I *hate* chess!"

"No smoking, no talking during the movie, and just one trip to the restroom. Have a nice flight."

"Your honor, he's leading the witness."

"The course record is 19."

"They don't hear so good when they
get old."

"He's only buying me a dishwasher to
save himself work."

"You don't want to infect all the other patients, do you?"

"What would you do if you swore to keep a secret and it was driving you crazy?"

"It's not working."

"I don't have to take off my clothes, do I?"

HERMAN

by JIM UNGER

THIS IS A VERY SAD CASE.

LADIES AND GENTLEMEN OF THE JURY...

UNLIKE YOURSELVES, MY CLIENT GREW UP WITHOUT THE ADVANTAGES OF INTELLIGENCE..

...CHARM...

...AND GOOD LOOKS.

"Do you want to know what's wrong with you or just the dollar amount?"

"I know there's more pleasure in giving. I like to suffer."

"Anyone sitting here?"

"The doctor says you'll still be able to play the piano."

"We're looking for someone honest, hardworking, and totally devoid of ambition."

"I knew you'd be back."

"We only have to empty it once a month."

"I may have to ruin your coat."

"Maurice, love is not blind enough to allow me to ignore that tie."

"Do you sell birthday cakes by the slice?"

"I took it to the wrong apartment."

HERMAN

by JIM UNGER

"I don't want you bringing your domestic problems to work."

"He's been teaching me to drive."

"I can hear the sea!"

"I can't read your writing!"

"You have to do your own dishes."

"Ambulance or not, Sunshine, *you* left the scene of an accident."

"My cousin, Irene, knows a good lawyer."

"Instead of taking me to an expensive dinner, can I have the money?"

"I guess your job's safe for a few
more weeks."

"How big are your safety deposit boxes?"

"Open your mouth."

"Be careful what you say around him.
He's not as dumb as he looks."

"He always does that when he's hungry."

"Got a 38-inch waist in dark gray?"

"Does that look like a non-stick frying pan to you?"

"Avoid all the hassles of remote control."

"You've got two choices: Quit smoking and drinking, or get a better-paying job."

"Get 'em before they come in the house."

"This one comes with a lifetime guarantee."

"Double cheese, with 'Happy Birthday' in mushrooms."

"I can't be any fairer than that — $1.5 million reduced to $25."

"Don't keep complaining about my mother."

"The previous owner was 10 feet tall."

"Smoking or non-smoking?"

HERMAN

by JIM UNGER

"Take me to my house. I want to order a large pepperoni."

"We're waiting for a probation report, Your Honor."

"You idiot! You threw away the keys to the washroom again!"

"I'll be wearing a pink carnation."

"You've been putting on damp clothing."

"You wouldn't last five minutes where I come from."

"He's not very sociable."

"First, a light dusting of defoliant."

"They know it's feeding time in 10 minutes."

"He's so lazy. He bought himself an exercise car."

"Settle an argument. How do you pronounce his name?"

HERMAN

by JIM UNGER

"Someone spilled a bottle this morning."

"Look at that rustproofing."

"Not the *laundry!*"

"You're exactly the same size as me."

"They knew how to build skeletons in those days."

"Her sister's making 10 bucks a week."

"The doctor says your cast can come off as soon as you've paid."

"I asked you a year ago to get me some help pulling up that drawbridge."

"Got any tools that float?"

"*Steak*, you idiot! Rare *steak*!"

"'Catch of the day' is off till the fog clears."

"Take the next left ... and what's the capital of Yugoslavia?"

HERMAN

by JIM UNGER

SOME SCIENTIST HAS INVENTED A PILL THAT MAKES YOU FEEL HAPPY.

IT'S NON-ADDICTIVE AND HAS NO SIDE EFFECTS

43 COUNTRIES HAVE BANNED IT.

"I want to send this birthday card to my brother, c.o.d."

"It's getting too commercial."

"They should move Christmas to January — everything's cheaper."

"Who ordered the chicken burger?"

"Stay alert. They've tripled the import duty on wallpaper."

"Make sure you hand that pass back before you leave the building."

"That's guaranteed waterproof to 100 fathoms."

"You've got enough in there for two weeks."

"It's time we heard from the silent majority."

"I told you it didn't smell."

"Well, now you know what my ex-husband looks like."

"He fetched it upside down again."

HERMAN

by JIM UNGER

WE'VE DECIDED TO USE AERIAL PHOTOGRAPHY.

"He sure looks forward to your
weekly visits."

"We want two round-trip tickets to here."

"It's picked me again."

"I had a good job waiting for me on the
outside, but they installed a
burglar alarm."

"I'll meet you in about an hour."

"Now don't worry about the noise this drill makes."

"Put these oven mitts on."

"It's a buck-fifty for 14 hours."

"Turn left at the light, and it's the 79th street on the right."

"We want something to match our carpet. What have you got with cigarette burns?"

"For what we are about to receive, thanks for nothing."

HERMAN

by JIM UNGER

"Get lost, lady. I'm looking for the X-ray department."

"Gustav will show you to your room."

"I think you ordered us a three-course meal from the wine list."

"Do you want me to close the window?"

"George thinks they should consider releasing a few human beings back into the wild."

"You want to test both eyes, don't you?"

"I would like to ask for your daughter's handmaiden."

"If I had to guess, I'd say a very large horsefly."

"Do you want the 75 cents or not?"

"My ex-husband said he'll pay for our wedding *and* the honeymoon."

"Do I look stupid? Of course you can marry my daughter."